TheOtherRoom
at Porter's

The Story
by Tess Berry-Hart

T0347997

CAST:
V: Hannah McPake
X: Siwan Morris
The Storyteller: Luciana Trapman

CREATIVES:
Writer: Tess Berry-Hart
Director: David Mercatali
Designer: Delyth Evans
Lighting Designer: Katy Morison
Sound Designer/Composer: Tic Ashfield
Video Designer: Simon Clode
Production Manager: Rhys Williams
Stage Manager: Rachel Bell
Season Fight Director: Kev McCurdy
Fight Choreographer: Cristian Cardenas
Associate Director: Matthew Holmquist
Assistant Director: Samantha Jones
Casting Director: Nicola Reynolds
Choreographer: Deborah Light
BSL Interpreter: Julie Doyle
Set Builder: Will Goad
Production Photographer: Kirsten McTernan

FRONT COVER IMAGE:
Photography: Simon Clode
Design: Limegreentangerine

The Story was first performed at The Other Room, Cardiff from 08/10/2019 – 27/10/2019. It was commissioned and produced as a part of The Violence Series.

The OtherRoom
at Porter's

Artistic Director & CEO: Dan Jones
Producer: George Soave
Associate Director: Matthew Holmquist
Trainee Director: Nerida Bradley
Trainee Producer: Ben Clark
Press & Marketing Associate: Alys Hewitt
Executive Producers: Dan Porter & David Wilson

The Other Room at Porter's is Cardiff's pub theatre. It was founded by Artistic Director Kate Wasserberg and Executive Director Bizzy Day in response to the exciting opportunity to develop an audience for drama in the heart of Cardiff. An intense, purpose-built space with 47 seats, The Other Room produces great modern plays and new work by and with Welsh, Wales-based and Wales-trained artists. The Other Room has fast established a reputation for quality and daring drama, won Fringe Theatre of the Year at the 2016, Stage Awards, and a plethora of accolades at The Wales Theatre Awards in 2015, 2016 and 2017. The theatre was shortlisted in the Arts category of the Cardiff Life Awards 2017 and 2018, as well as for the prestigious Peter Brook Empty Space Award, 2017. The Other Room is currently run by Artistic Director and CEO, Dan Jones.

The Other Room would also like to thank Andrew Havers, Arad Goch, Arts Council England, Arts Council of Wales, Fiona & Norman Bell, The Carne Trust, Cathy Boyce, Chapter Arts Centre, Claire Bottomley, David Bond, Emily Pearce, Emma Evans, Emma West, The Esmee Fairbairn Foundation, The Garfield Weston Foundation, Geraldine Lamb, Hayley Burns, Heather Davies, Keynsham & Saltford DAA, The Leche Trust, Merrial Knight, Michael Carklin, National Theatre Wales, Philip Carne, Pontio Arts and Innovation Centre, Porter's, Prysg, Royal Welsh College of Music and Drama, Theatr Clwyd, Theatrau Sir Gâr, Theatre503, Theatre Genedlaethol Cymru, University of South Wales, Wales Millennium Centre and Yasmin Williams.

The Story was made possible by the incredible work of founding Executive Director, **Bizzy Day** – whose work as Executive Director, Producer and Fundraiser made this play a reality.

When I was asked by The Other Room, Cardiff, whether I would write a play for their planned 2019 Violence Season, I didn't have to think twice. The theme chimed perfectly with something I had been wanting to write about for some time. Since 2015, I had spent time volunteering in the Calais Jungle, as well as refugee camps in Lesvos and Athens, and had witnessed with dismay the backlash against the refugee crisis evidencing itself as growing nationalism, hard borders and rising right-wing sentiment across Europe. As well as seeing my own friends and colleagues in the volunteer effort criminalised and charged for pulling drowning people out of the sea or handing out food, I was affected by the words that media and politicians used to alienate and distort reality; whether it be dehumanising expressions such as "swarms of migrants," or the rousing and divisive rhetoric of "traitors" or "enemies of the people." This violence of language – the way in which words were used to narrow perspective, reduce compassion towards others, and co-opt the narrative of events to the extent of taking away the understanding of humanity itself – needed to be told; and after a few conversations with Dan Jones the artistic director, *The Story* was born.

My greatest love and thanks to The Other Room, Cardiff, for believing in me enough to be part of this amazing season, especially to Dan for taking a punt on me in the first place and for their ambition in commissioning and staging three new plays to explore violence in its various forms.

My endless gratitude and love to all the creatives on the show; David the director for always intuitively knowing what I meant before I mean it and for creating such beauty out of my scattered thoughts; our brilliant cast Siwan, Hannah and Luciana for breathing life into my characters to bring them into such weird and wonderful glory, Del for her incredible set, Tic for her searing soundscapes, Simon for his next-level audio-visual and Katy for her lighting magic.

Thank you also to the team behind the scenes; Nicola for masterminding our brilliant cast, Rachel and Sam for their everlasting patience and boundless ability to save the day, as well as a huge thank you to Rhys, Deborah, Will, and Julie who brought together their talents to make *The Story* happen. Finally my thanks to the fabulous and tireless team of people at TOR who have put the Violence Series together; George, Matthew, Nerida, Ben and Alys.

WRITER: Tess Berry-Hart

Tess is a playwright and activist living in Wales, and was recently shortlisted for the inaugural BBC Wales/NTW Writer in Residence 2019 award.

Tess's theatre credits include: *Cargo* (2016); about refugees travelling in a cargo container (Arcola Theatre, London); which has been translated into Turkish and toured by the Turkish National Theatre (2018 – 2019); and two verbatim plays, *Someone To Blame* (2012); about a miscarriage of justice (King's Head Theatre); and *Sochi* (2014); about the anti-gay propaganda laws in Russia (Hope Theatre London and the Edinburgh Festival). Benefit gala performances of Sochi have also been produced in New York and Los Angeles. Tess is also a founder member of refugee charities Calais Action and the Citizens of the World Choir and has volunteered in Northern France, Lesvos and Athens.

CAST:

V: Hannah McPake

For The Other Room: *Seanmhair*.

Other recent theatre credits include: *The Shape Of The Pain* (China Plate); *Double Vision* (Wales Millennium Centre); *The Flop* (Spymonkey/Hijinx); *Alice In Wonderland*; *Wind In The Willows*; *Cinders*; *Plum, And Me Will*; *Maudie's Rooms* (Sherman Theatre); *I Am Thomas* (Told By An Idiot/Nts); *Rapunzel* (Citizens Theatre); *The Tempest* (Improbable/Northern Stage); *The Gamblers* (Greyscale/ Dundee Rep); *Romeo And Juliet, Knight Of The Burning Pestle* (Shakespeare's Globe); *Wonderman*; *Silly Kings*; *Green Man//Red Woman* (National Theatre Wales); *The Forsythe Sisters* and *The Bloody Ballad* (Gagglebabble).

TV and film credits include: *Trollied for Sky* and *Skins Series V for E4.*

Radio credits include: *Seven Songs For Simon Dixelius* and *Modesty Blaise* for BBC Radio 4.

X: Siwan Morris

Siwan trained at Manchester Metropolitan University School of Theatre.

Theatre credits include: *Thick As Thieves* (Cleanbreak/Theatre Clwyd); *Dublin Carol* (Sherman Theatre); *Highway One* (Wales Millennium Centre); *Bird* (Royal Exchange/Sherman Theatre); *Violence And Son* (Royal Court Theatre); *Tonypandemonium* (National Theatre Wales); *Good Night Out In The Valleys* (National Theatre Wales); *Cloakroom* (Sherman Theatre); *Midsummer Nights Dream* (Theatre Clwyd); *Knives In Hens* (Theatre Royal Bath); *Suddenly Last Summer* (Theatre Clwyd); *The Seagull* (Bristol Old Vic); *Much Ado About Nothing/Twelfth Night* (Rj Williamson Uk Tour); *The Winters Tale/Merchant Of Venice* (Ludlow Theatre Festival); *Feast Of Snails* (Lyric Theatre); *Equus, Rape Of The Fair Country, Hosts Of Rebecca, Journey Of Mary Kelly, The Rabbit* and *Christmas Carol* (Theatre Clwyd).

TV credits include: *Gwaith Catref, Pishyn Glo, Caerdydd, Con Passionata* (S4c); *Eastenders, Doctor Who, Our Girl, Wolfblood, Holby City, Casualty, Whites* (BBC); *Belonging, Tales From Pleasure Beach, The Bench* (BBC Wales); *Miss Marple, Mine All Mine* (ITV); *Skins* (Channel 4) and *Mind To Kill* (HTV).

Film credits include: *No Vacancies, Dark Signal, Desperate Measures, The Devils Vice, The Machine, Sister Lulu* and *Sucker Fish*.

The Storyteller: Luciana Trapman

Luciana trained for four years in her home country of The Netherlands and another three at the Royal Welsh College of Music and Drama. In 2018 she was a contestant for the Spotlight Showcase Prize.

Theatre credits include: *Extinct* (Yello Brick); *Les Miserablés* (August 012) and *Robinson: The Other Island* (Give It A Name).

CREATIVES:

Director: David Mercatali

David is a theatre director based in Cardiff.

Credits include: *God Of Chaos* (Theatre Royal Plymouth); *Tremor* (Sherman, Edinburgh Fringe, 59E59 NYC); *Buddy* (Sherman, Gate, RWCMD); *Blue Heart* (Orange Tree/Tobacco Factory); *Tonight with Donny Stixx* (Edinburgh Fringe/Bunker); *Cargo; Insignificance* (Arcola); *Radiant Vermin* (Soho Theatre, Tobacco Factory, 59E59 NYC); *Radieuse Vermine* (Theatre Montparnasse, Festival de Avignon); *Little Light* (Orange Tree); *Every You Every Me* (Salisbury Playhouse); *Dark Vanilla Jungle* (Soho Theatre, Edinburgh Fringe, National Tour *Fringe First Winner); *Feathers in the Snow; Johnny Got His Gun; Our Ajax* (Southwark Playhouse); *Coolatully; Black Jesus* (Finborough); *Sochi 2014* (Hope Theatre); *Tender Napalm* (Southwark Playhouse, National Tour); *Someone to Blame* (King's Head Theatre); *Moonfleece* (Riverside Studios).

Designer: Delyth Evans

Delyth trained at The Royal Welsh College of Music and Drama, graduating in 2018.

Recent credits include: *American Nightmare* (The Other Room); *How We Begin* (King's Head Theatre); *One Giant Leap* (Brockley Jack); *In Lipstick* (The Pleasance Theatre); *Out Of Love* (LAMDA); *All That* (King's Head Theatre) and *Punk Rock* (RWCMD).

Lighting Designer: Katy Morison

Katy is a Lighting Designer based in South Wales. She has recently worked on *American Nightmare* by Matthew Bulgo, the first play in the VIOLENCE Season at Cardiff's The Other Room; as well as *Shooting Rabbits/Saethu* Cwningod by Powderhouse and *Woof* at Sherman Theatre. Her work in 2018 included *Exodus* for Wales-based company Motherlode and follows from the success of *The Good Earth*, which received 5-star reviews and enjoyed an off-Broadway run in New York to critical acclaim. She also designed three shows as part of National Theatre Wales' NHS70 season.

She has worked as an associate and Re-lighter, as well as Lighting Designer for Venue 13 at the Edinburgh Fringe, and also as a Production Supervisor and lighting tutor at Royal Welsh College of Music and Drama.

She was a member of the Production Team at Sherman Cymru for over seven years.

Sound Designer/Composer: Tic Ashfield

Tic Ashfield MMus BMus (Hons) (RWCMD) is a BAFTA Cymru Award Winning Composer and Sound Designer based in South Wales. She has created music and sound for numerous projects including work for film, TV, theatre, dance, animation, installation and educational outreach projects.

Commissioners and collaborators include: BBC 1 Wales, BBC 2, BBC 4, S4C, All3Media, Fiction Factory, Severn Screen, John Hardy Music, Creative Assembly, National Theatre Wales,

The Other Room Theatre, Taking Flight Theatre, Chippy Lane Productions, Omidaze Productions, Winding Snake Productions, Welsh National Opera, Lighthouse Theatre, Joio and Gwyn Emberton Dance.

As a composer and sound designer she focuses on using a combination of found sound manipulation and sampling, synthesis and instrumental writing to create bespoke soundworlds, often within collaborative settings.

Video Designer: Simon Clode

Simon is an artist/ filmmaker whose work intercuts many disciplines, with interests lying in ethnographic, environmental and global political commentary. His films have screened in competition at BAFTA qualifying festivals such as Aesthetica Short Film Festival. He has been a video designer on numerous projects for national and international theatre and dance, as well as working on large scale site-specific work like *The Tide Whisperer* and *Now the Hero*. Arts Council Wales supports his artist films with his most recent film installation showing at Palestine's contemporary Arts Festival 'Qalandiya International'. He is currently one of the directors selected for the BFI Network / BAFTA GURU 2019/2020 program, as well as being a BFI Horizons recipient.

Production Manager: Rhys Williams

Rhys worked in the Audio Visual industry for over 25 years with responsibilities in deploying worldwide systems and solutions to many corporate giants. In 2018 Rhys decided to change career to follow his passion in the Theatre and Live Events. Since making that decision, Rhys has undertaken a Master's Degree at the Royal Welsh College of Music and Drama in Stage and Event Management. Rhys has worked on many Theatrical and Live Events, most recently Simon Stephens' *Rage* and Matthew Bulgo's *American Nightmare*. From technical deployment to process administration, Rhys brings a multitude of skill sets to his Production Management.

Stage Manager: Rachel Bell

Rachel has recently graduated from Bristol Old Vic Theatre School after studying Professional Stage Management. Whilst at the Theatre School, she was SM on the Nativity schools tour, DSM on *Poison*, *Let The Right One In* and *Kiss Me*, and ASM on *The Elephant Man*. She was a part of British Youth Opera's season in 2018, working as DSM on *The Enchanted Island*. Since leaving the theatre school, she has worked as ASM for *Eugene Onegin* at Buxton International Festival and SM on the book for *The Mullah of Downing Street* at Chipping Norton Theatre.

Fight Director: Kev McCurdy

Kev is an Equity professional Fight Director. He primarily trained as an actor at The Royal Welsh College of Music and Drama from 1991 – 1998. He gained his Equity Professional Fight Directors status in 1996. Kev has been Royal Welsh Colleges' resident fight tutor since 2005 and has worked on a variety of stage, tv and film projects around the UK and abroad. Kev was also very honoured to have been awarded The Paddy Crean Fight Award at the event four years ago. He was also awarded the RWCMD Fellowship award two years ago. He's also the Co-Founder and Chairman for The Academy of Performance Combat. Kev has worked on numerous plays, tv shows, operas, video games and feature films. Some companies he has worked for: Walt Disney, Pixar, Atlas Entertainment, RSC, National Theatre, Old Vic, Young Vic, Shakespeare's Globe, Curve Theatre, Manchester Royal Exchange, BBC, Sky 1, ITV, Channel 4, S4C Wales, Sega.

Associate Director: Matthew Holmquist

Matthew is the current Associate Director at The Other Room Theatre as well as Artistic Director of Red Oak Theatre.

Directing credits include: *Cardiff Boy* (Red Oak Theatre, The Other Room); *A Recipe for Sloe Gin* (Clocktower Theatre, World of Boats); *Blue Stockings* (Sherman Players, Sherman Theatre); *The River* (Red Oak Theatre, Loco Bristol) and *We Had a Black Dog* (Red Oak Theatre, Theatre De Menilmontant, Paris).

Associate Director/Staff Director credits include: *Eugene Onegin* (Buxton Opera); *Le Vin Herbe*, *Don Giovanni* (Welsh National Opera / Opera Cenedlaethol Cymru) and *A Christmas Carol* (Simply Theatre, Geneva).

Assistant Director credits include: *Tremor*, *Taming of The Shrew* (Sherman Theatre); *Simplicius Simplicissimus* (Independent Opera); *Insignificance* (Theatre Clwyd); *Kommilitonen!* (Welsh National Youth Opera / Opera Ieuenctid Cenedlaethol Cymru).

Assistant Director: Samantha Jones

Sam is an emerging Theatre Director based in South Wales. Sam trained as an actor at East 15 Acting School, working and touring in London and around the UK. Whilst living in London Sam Co-owned and directed Musical Youth London where she directed numerous amateur productions such as *Les Miserables*, *Sweeney Todd* and *Little Shop of Horrors* to name a few. Sam also co-runs Taffire Theatre, a Welsh based theatre company. When Sam returned to Wales she embarked on her director training as Trainee Director at The Other Room which spring boarded her into her directing career. Sam also works with Timothy Howe at the Sherman Theatre & their high-quality youth programme.

Credits include: *Road*, Jim Cartwright RWCMD (Assistant Director to Michael Fentiman); *Rage*, Simon Stephens RWCMD (Associate Director to Elle While); *Crave*, Sarah Kane The Other Room (Director); *Trailing Rhiannon*, Emma Watkins R&D Chapter Arts with Little Minute Theatre (Director); *Tithonus*, Matthew Bulgo R&D Sherman Theatre (Assistant Director to Matthew Holmquist, Red Oak Theatre); and *Small Fry*, Hannah Lad Pop Factory, Porth (Director).

Tess Berry-Hart

THE STORY

OBERON BOOKS
LONDON

WWW.OBERONBOOKS.COM

First published in 2019 by Oberon Books Ltd
521 Caledonian Road, London N7 9RH
Tel: +44 (0) 20 7607 3637 / Fax: +44 (0) 20 7607 3629
e-mail: info@oberonbooks.com
www.oberonbooks.com

A catalogue record for this book is available from the British Library.

PB ISBN: 9781786829344
E ISBN: 9781786829351

Photography: Simon Clode
Design: Limegreentangerine

10 9 8 7 6 5 4 3 2 1

Characters

X, a volunteer (male)

V, an interrogator (female)

THE STORYTELLER

THE STORYTELLER: I'm going to tell you a story.

It's not a bedtime story. It's not for those who are afraid of the dark.

It doesn't have a happy ending. Or it might do. We'll see.

The beauty of it is that it changes in the telling,

Depending on who you are and what you're hearing,

A dance where you don't know who's leading,

A way that keeps changing,

Where your story is your only passport.

And when you arrive, it's a strange country,

Where you don't speak the language and you learn like an infant,

Babbling and clicking, words squeezed from chaos

Through an untrained throat; a rusty voice

Mirroring the lips in front of you, copying those strange sounds,

An unspeakable alphabet, struggling to please

Over and over again

Until you hear it.

"Good. Good. You're doing very well.

Now tell us what happened next."

SNAP LIGHTS

SCENE 1

A room with two chairs and a spotlight.

X sits on one of the chairs, dressed in travelling clothes, exhausted and uneasy, flicking through a sheaf of papers. Yawns. Pause. We hear the tick of a clock.

V enters, dressed in some kind of official-looking uniform, harassed.

V: Ugh, I'm sorry. You've been waiting ages. Queue's so long today, we're getting through it as fast as we can.

X: That's okay, I –

V: Need anything? A drink, something to eat?

X: Umm, maybe a –

V: Great, well we'll dive straight in then. *(Draws up chair, sits.)* Now I've got a copy of your border entry application here, and so we, The People, have to ask you a few questions; it's protocol really, but you know, always better to be safe than sorry.

X: Of course.

V: *(Scans file.)* So you are of The People originally?

X: Yes

V: Yes. Good. And you have spent the last year … *(Squints, reads.)* "travelling in the annexed territories for humanitarian reasons?"

X: The – occupied territories, yes.

V: Yes. Wonderful. And the purpose of your entry here today.

X: I – well, I'm back now, my wife's here to pick me up.

V: Your wife?

X: Yes.

V: Lovely. Married long?

X: Five years, something like that.

V: Your wife is of The People too?

X: Yes.

V: Occupation?

X: Well, everything outside the border has been illegally occupied so –

V: I meant, your occupation?

X: Ah, I don't really have one now.

V: What did you use to do?

X: Oh, uh, insurance clerk, nothing exciting.

V: Children?

X: Uh, two. My wife's. From her first marriage.

V: Amazing. I've got two as well. Boys. Little terrors. Let me guess. You look like the type who has boys. No? Yes!

X: Well, we've got one boy, one –

V: Long time to be apart, no? A whole year?

X: It wasn't – it wasn't intentional.

V: No?

X: Well, it was just meant to be a few months, but when I got out there, and *saw* – I felt needed, really *needed* out there, so –

V: Yes. Fantastic. Did you see, um, the mountains? That mountain range everyone always talks about?

X: Ah I didn't go that far north.

V: I'd love to see that when all the trouble is over. Apparently amazing in the sunrise. The whole mountain is pink. You can't tell where the sky ends and … no. Where you begin and … No. Where you end and the sky begins! Real out of body experience, they say. You're so lucky.

X: Uh, I didn't actually –

V: I can't do camping. The whole beans-on-toast and gnats in your knickers thing. Destroys the mystique.

X: Oh, haha, yeah.

V: I imagine you had to do a lot of camping.

X: Uh, well, you have to, there's no actual –

V: Couldn't do that. Not at all.

X: Yeah, okay, yeah.

V: Incredible. So let's press on, this is the awkward bit, I have to read this in full so we can do some box-ticking; it's a bit of a mouthful, but anyway *(Reads airily.)* "Are you now, or have you ever been, engaged in any activity or plans which could compromise, destabilise or otherwise threaten the security of The People, their citizens, institutions or democracy, now or in the future?"

X: No.

V: No. Great. And what exactly did you do during your year spent *(Reads.)* "travelling in the annexed territories."

X: Uhhhh … occupied, well, relief assistance, mainly.

V: Relief assistance.

X: Giving out food, blankets, non-food items. Shoes. Lots of shoes. I mean, there's thousands of –

V: So *(Scribbling.)* more exactly, "providing relief assistance to displaced persons in the annexed territories."

X: Yes, mainly, the –

V: Mainly. And the other times?

Pause.

X: You know, it's the strangest thing. I keep thinking – I'm sure we've – I'm sure we've met before.

V: No! Really?

X: Yes! Your face is so familiar.

V: No way! That's incredible.

X: It's like – like we've known each other for ages.

V: How curious. I've only been in the job a few months.

X: No really, I … honestly, it's uncanny … ah, it's going to drive me mad, now –

V: I see a lot of familiar faces every day but then I've got a really good eye. I never forget a face; you know, the way an eyebrow tilts up, the way someone holds their head – it's all in here. A super-recogniser, they call me, and I'm fairly certain we've never –

X: Ah – hang on, it's coming – no, it's gone again.

V: *(Charmingly.)* And – the other times?

X: I'm sorry?

V: The other times. That you weren't *(Reads.)* "providing humanitarian assistance to displaced persons in the annexed territories."

X: The occupied – uhh, sorry I don't quite –

V: You previously stated to The People that *(Checks notes.)* "*mainly* you were providing –"

X: Oh I see, I mean, okay sometimes I travelled about, to see the country, or watched the protests –

V: You watched the protests –

X: Yes, well there's a lot, isn't there, especially after the shooting at –

V: Assist at the protests in any capacity?

X: Me? Oh no.

V: Distribute material, flyers, anything like that?

X: No, like I said –

V: Carry a package for anyone, maybe?

X: I only meant, the protests were everywhere so sometimes we couldn't even get the food truck through otherwise we'd get mobbed, and then there'd be all the gas, and the police –

V: Associate with any of the protestors?

X: *(Very slight uncertainty.)* Well, I suppose I would see a few familiar faces –

V: Familiar faces?

There's an indiscernible shift of tension in the air. X chooses her words carefully.

X: I mean, not – friends, just maybe I'd have seen them in the soup line the night before, for instance, I didn't personally know –

V: Not friends of yours, then.

X: No, no, absolutely most definitely not, friends.

V: Wonderful. So you class yourself as having provided solely humanitarian assistance in the annexed territories then.

X: The – Yes.

V: *(Writing.)* Solely … humanitarian … Yes. *(Smiling.)* Fantastic. OK! I think we're done here.

X: *(Relaxing.)* Oh good. Thank you.

V: And on that note, and very unfortunately, I'm sorry to tell you that your preliminary application for border crossing to The People has been rejected.

Beat.

X: … Excuse me?

V: *(After a pause, repeating.)* And on that note, and very unfortunately, I'm sorry to tell you –

X: I heard, *rejected,* but – but on what grounds?

V: Confidential, I'm afraid. *(Anticipating X's protest.)* The grounds for rejection will be supplied directly to a senior Voice for investigation, whereupon you will have the opportunity to discuss your situation –

X: I don't understand.

V: At present, you are not permitted to rejoin The People, so you will be held in temporary detention while an investigation is carried out.

X: But. I – live here.

V: *Lived* here.

X: What? I was born here, this is my home, my wife is just the other side of that – she just texted me now, she's been waiting here for hours –

V: Listen –

X: My mother, my cousins, my dog, my family, my friends, my flat – everything is here, everything of mine, everything of me –

V: Hey, hey. Calm down. It's just one of those "computer says no" issues.

X: What computer? How does a non-existent computer say no?

V: So what it is, right, people always get worried and freak out, right, just like you're doing now, so I'll explain. Your application has brought up a redflag so a superior Voice will have to ask you a few more questions.

X: What redflag? What quest – ?

V: Happens all the time. Absolutely nothing to worry about. Better to be safe than sorry. The Voice will be in to see you shortly.

(Rises, turns.) Just one tip; keep calm.

X: I am calm!

V: Good. Because, you know, stress doesn't look good.

X: Well I am a bit stressed, because –

V: I'm just saying this because I like you. I think you're a good person, and –

X: I am a good person!

V: Of course. I mean, I can tell, but it's the optics of the thing, you know.

X: Huh?

V: If there's nothing to hide, then why would you be stressed?

X weighs this up.

X: Okay.

V: Deep breaths. Perfect. Remember; eye contact, but not too
   much, otherwise it'll look a bit creepy.

X: Um.

V: Try not to fidget, or scratch. Keep your body language
   relaxed and open, but not stiff, you don't want to come
   across as artificial.

X: Thanks.

V: And one last tip; get your story straight.

X: What story? I don't have a story.

V: I mean, just, tell the truth.

X: Of course.

V: Exactly as it happened. Okay?

X: *(Bewildered.)* Okay?

V: That's the spirit. Chin up.

   V turns to go. X sits up.

X: Wait. I've got it.

V: What?

X: Did you ever go to – to the camp at Llanrhaeadr?

V: Me? No. *(Laughs.)*

X: Really?

V: Never in my life. I'm of the People, through and through.
   Never been to the annexed territories, probably never will.

X: So odd. I could have sworn.

V: Probably the uniform. We all look the same to you guys, huh.

X: Haha, um.

V: Anyway. Break a leg.

V snaps fingers at X and gives a thumbs up in encouragement, exits.

SNAP LIGHTS

THE STORYTELLER: We are the people the will of the people
the voice of the people the people know what they want
it's democracy an enemy of democracy is an enemy
of the people the voice of the people is everything we
speak through them they speak for us we control them
they represent us that's democracy it's a coup against the
people the people are rising up the people will not be
crushed the people are sovereign –

SNAP LIGHTS

SCENE 2

X paces back and forth, talking on the phone.

X: But that's just it, I don't know how long they're – *(Pause.)*
I know, I know, it's, well, you know what they're like. I'm
a bit worried now. I should never have mentioned those
fucking protests.

Do you want to go back home and wait there with the
kids? I don't know when I'll be out at this rate. I'll ring
you – okay someone's outside, I have to go. Yes. You too.
Everything's going to be okay.

*V enters with a box, dressed in military fatigues. Her demeanour
and attitude are markedly different. X puts phone away and stares
at V, relieved.*

X: Oh! You're back!

V puts the box on the table and stands to attention.

X: I'm glad it's you, I was expecting –

V: Remove all loose items and jewellery and put them in the box please.

X: Um –

V: Any watches, rings, earrings, wallet, keys, phone.

X: My phone?

V: All loose items please.

X: But why?

V: They'll be analysed while we conduct the next section of your interview.

X: Analysed? But –

V: Please take off your shoes also, any scarves, belts, laces or other accessories.

X: Wait, what's happening? You just – you just told me there was nothing to worry about.

V: In the box please.

X: But –

V: Refusal to comply at this stage may be interpreted as criminal obstruction of democratic justice and treated accordingly.

X: I'm not – I just –

V: Are you obstructing The People in their democratic investigation into issues of national security?

X: No. No of course not.

V: In the box please.

X: Can – can I ring my wife? Just, quickly?

V: The quicker you do this, the quicker the necessary
investigations will be.

*X uneasily removes accessories one by one and puts them hesitantly
in the box.*

V: Shirt and trousers too please.

X: Why –

V: All external clothing needs to be analysed by forensics.

X: Forensics?

V: Are you obstructing –

X: Okay, okay.

Pause.

X: Can I – I mean, do I get any privacy?

V turns round and folds arms, waiting.

*X unwillingly removes outer clothes and puts them in a box; she's
left in just a T-shirt and pants.*

V: Thank you. Arms up and open please, feet two paces apart
(Frisks X briskly in a pat-down.) Turn around please, can
you part your hair for me?

X: Uh – okay.

V: Turn around again, please. Had any dental work done in
the past year?

X: Any …? No

V: Tongue out, please *(Shines flashlight into X's mouth.)* Okay
so I'm going to take a swab from the inside of your cheek,

it's a non-invasive procedure that will be cross-matched on The People's database of known criminal enemy profiles, do you give your consent for this?

X: Well, hang on, I –

V: Do you give your consent to The People to perform their necessary and democratic investigation into matters of public security?

X: I think, aren't there laws about this, ways to –

V: Are you obstructing The People's necessary and democratic –

X: No, no, of course I'm not obstructing –

V: Do you give your consent or –

X: I'm just – is this really needed?

V: Is there any reason that you would withhold consent to The People?

X: No, yes, okay.

V: You're giving your consent?

X: Yes, yes, I consent.

V: You are giving your full and free consent, such consent not having been obtained by force, duress or misrepresentation, and you are of sound mind and in full possession of your faculties today...?

Pause.

X: Yes, okay, fine.

X opens mouth, V takes a swab.

V: Thank you. Take a seat please.

V takes the swab and the box of X's possessions out of the room.

Pause. X sits barefooted and uncertain, crosses arms and draws knees up.

V returns with a red boilersuit.

V: Put this on, please.

X: But –

V: Put this on.

X: I'm – I'm not a prisoner, I –

V: You don't have to wear it.

V makes as if to take it away, X grabs it, stares at it, unwillingly puts it on.

X: When will I get my phone back?

V: Do you have particular need of your phone at the present time?

X: I just – well –

V: You seem tense.

X: I'm not tense. *(Pause, X catches V staring, uncrosses arms and looks relaxed with an effort.)* It's just, you get used to having your phone with you, don't you. These days.

V: Anything of concern on it?

X: On my phone? No, but –

V: But?

X: ....

V: If there's anything to tell us about any incriminating content stored on your phone, then now would be your chance.

X sighs.

V: Do you possess any image or communication on your phone which is of threat to the democracy, institutions or public safety of The People?

X: OK *(Laughs.)* it's nothing like that. It's just there's – private stuff on there.

V: Private stuff.

X: Well, you know.

V: When the safety of The People is at risk, nothing is private.

X: Uhhhh –

V: Do you possess any image or communication –

X: Look, OK! *(Laughs nervously.)* Pictures, you know, the kind couples take, okay that's all I just didn't want – anyone looking –

V: Anything not of threat to the democracy, institutions and public safety of The People will be disregarded for the purposes of this investigation.

X: Okay, thank you, okay.

V: You seem stressed.

X: I'm not stressed. *(Makes obvious effort to assume relaxed and open body language.)*

V: You're staring a lot.

X: I am?

V: A lot.

Pause. X looks down.

X: Shouldn't I – if this is an investigation, shouldn't there be someone else present?

V: Someone else?

X: I don't know, an observer? A lawyer?

V: Do you have reason to think you need a lawyer?

X: Well no, but –

V: Why would you need a lawyer?

X: I don't *need* a –

V: Have you done something that you'd need a lawyer for?

X: Of course not, but, I don't understand all this, you said you could tell I was a good person.

V: When did I say that?

X: Just – well, a few hours ago, when you checked my border application.

V: I think you must have confused me with someone else. We've never met before.

Beat.

X: Okay, well I'm confused now, we definitely –

V: We've never met before.

X: I know you must see a lot of people, but –

V: You're saying that I'm –

X: No, no, not at all.

V: Your case was referred to me because of your initial border refusal; I deal with investigations into national security.

X: *(Appalled.)* National security? But I'm just trying to get home.

V: While the investigation is conducted, you *are* a matter of national security.

X stares at V, then drops eyes.

X: I'd like a lawyer, please.

V: A lawyer.

X: Yes, well – things are getting difficult, and I think – I really think, I shouldn't be alone in this, I'd – I need –

V: You seem confused.

X: I – yes, I am, no, it's not confused exactly but I just think, it would be better to have a lawyer with me, so –

V: It would be better to have – ?

X: Yes, I'm not saying I've done anything, or did do, or – I'm going to do anything, but – I'm worried I'm going to say something that isn't the truth.

V: Why would you say anything that's not the truth?

X: I wouldn't – I mean, I wouldn't intend to, but, I feel tripped up, that's all I'm saying.

V: You think we're trying to trip you up?

X: Not intentionally, but there's these questions, all these questions, and I want to get my story straight.

V: Your story?

X: I mean the truth straight, the truth straight in my head, that's all –

V: May I remind you that you have previously declared to the People that you are not now, nor have ever been, engaged in any activity –

X: I, I remember, yes, it's nothing to do with that –

V: But you still need a lawyer.

X: I would – *like* one.

V: A lawyer will make things go much slower.

X: How much slower?

V: By a few days.

X: *(Panicked.)* A few days? I thought I'd be out by the end of the afternoon.

V: Not in cases of national security, I'm afraid.

X looks at V, catches V staring, drops eyes, meets them again, tries to look relaxed, agonises.

X: I'd still … like to speak to someone.

V: I'll see what I can do.

Exit V. X paces, waits. (It's a long wait.)

X: Hello? Hello?

There is no answer.

X sleeps. Wakes. Sleeps. Repeat.

SNAP LIGHTS

SCENE 3

V breezes in, dressed in business suit and carrying a briefcase. Different demeanour, pleasant but scatty, slightly not with it. A functioning alcoholic?

X wakes up, groggily, stiffens at the sight of her.

V: 'Scuse the hair, I got the call when I was in the shower, they said I had to come right away. Didn't even get time to blowdry *(Takes out papers, looks confused.)* Tattersen? Price?

X: Sorry?

V: Your name is Tattersen? *(X shakes head dumbly.)* Price? No? *(Checks papers.)* Have they sent me to the wrong place again?

X: No, no, it's me, remember, it's definitely me, I asked you for a lawyer, I've been waiting ages, days –

V: *(Thunderstruck.)* You asked me for –

X: I requested a lawyer, yes, yes.

V: *(Doubtfully.)* You are the Category X prisoner?

X: I – suppose so, yes.

V: Ahhhhh! Here you are, hiding! *(Extracts paper, tutting.)* Get here by twelve if you wanna get paid, who do they think they are, eh?

Pause. X stares at her.

V: Did I … ? Sorry, my glasses. Blind as a bat without them. *(Hunts around interminably.)* Ah that's better. OK. What do we have here. *(Reads, tutting, shakes head.)* Ah. Hmmm. Yes. Ohhhh. *(Looks concerned.)* No, no, no, that's not on at all.

X stands watching V anxiously.

V: These pro-bono cases, they wear you down. The things you see! Enough to retire anyone early. A young girl, my last one, trafficked by her own uncle. At least, she says it was her uncle, she's probably protecting her father. And another young guy, found cut open and kidneys taken out because the gang needed payment. Only last week! I mean, you have to laugh. Not because it's funny but – the things you see in my line of work, yeah, you have to laugh! *(Laughs.)* Don't you?

Pause.

V: Aaahhhh. I don't know. You have to laugh.

X: You're –

V: I'm your Voice. Appointed by The People, so you can be heard.

X: So – you're a lawyer too?

V: Too?

X: We – we've spoken before. A few days ago. I think it was a few days, I can't remember.

V: *(Utterly bewildered.)* We did?

X: Here. In this cell. We did.

V: I'm not sure I follow.

X: *(Carefully.)* Yes, you took my phone off me and –

V: Goodness. I'm sorry I really don't … You might have talked to one of my colleagues?

X: It wasn't – okay, I don't know. I just don't know any more.

V: Well I'm here now, lucky for you, and as I said, with you being classified as a Category X prisoner, I'm here to be *your* voice as a non-person, or, strictly legally, "an individual not of The People."

X: A non-person –

V: Well, to be of The People you cannot be an enemy of The People, and as someone under investigation it's up to you to prove your innocence, right.

X: I am – I *am* –

V: Oh! Wait! Have they read you the right to silence yet?

X: Um.

V: Ah now they really should have done that, at least. Naughty boys. Naughty, naughty boys. Never play by the book. I'm going to have to have a word with them about it.

X: But –

V: You have the right to remain silent, but if you don't remain silent, it can be used against you, as can your silence, if you don't say anything in your own defence.

X: I don't understand.

V: In essence, if you're guilty, then neither talking nor silence will save you. *(Smiles.)* Basically, in layman's terms, you're fucked either way.

X: What – what am I supposed to have done?

V: Straight down to brass tacks. No nonsense. I like it. Well, what we do know is this: You're being held on suspicion of criminality during your time in the annexed territories and so your right to be a part of The People has been revoked.

X: What!

V: *(Repeating.)* Well, what we do know is this: you're –

X: Yes, I got it, but – what criminality? What am I supposed to have done?

V: *(Shrugs.)* That's just it. *(Leans forward, confidentially.)* I can't get any more out of them because the Voice is always a right arsehole when it comes to giving facts, when it comes to court it can say, "oh no, I didn't say that" so we have to screw it for every little detail we can.

X: But surely – the Voice has to say what it is I did?

V: Honestly? The only important thing is for you to prove that you didn't.

X: Didn't what?

V: Do what you're accused of.

X: But I don't even know what I'm supposed to have done!

V: Well, that's the hard part.

X: So I've got to – defend myself against something that I don't know?

V: We've got to get your story straight.

X: My story is straight!

V: But you asked for me, so –

X: So? –

V: See how that looks?

X: Fuck, I mean, my story is the truth, so –

V: The truth. Excellent. Good start.

X: My story is really, really simple.

V: Really simple, good.

X: I'm a volunteer, a normal person –

V: How normal?

X: Very. Very normal.

V: Normal as in average intelligence, normal as in nothing special to look at, or normal as in –

X: Um, okay, just a normal life I mean, I used to work in an office, just processing insurance applications, it was boring, really, and when I heard about all the trouble out there, it felt like – it felt like something I could do, you know? To help?

V: You felt you could be something. Someone.

X: So I just went out, in Llanrhaeadr camp, since it all started, I just gave out food and patched up people when they got hurt for a while, and then I came home.

V: *(Holding up hand.)* Ok, wait, the way out of this thing is not that you tell us what it is that you've done, but it's very important that it counters what their story is about you first.

X: *(Confused.)* What is –

V: See, it's all a card game. We're not searching out the truth of the matter, no, we leave all that to the scientists. What we're doing here, it's entertainment. Storytelling. Salesmanship. Whose story is more compelling to The People. Can you move them, make them feel, make them think, win them round?

X: I – uh –

V: The Voice's story is a royal flush, so our story has to be a full suit of aces. Wham bang, double-flush, their suit chucked out and the croupier hands you the money, the casino doors open and everyone in the place is checking the CCTV and wondering how on earth you pulled it off.

X: You mean –

V: What is truth these days? Come on! You have to show that your story is more true than theirs –

X: But how can there be two truths?

V: It's all about the narrative. Will The People believe you over a Senior Voice? Are you in fact, a normal person? Or is your normality actually a sinister thing, a cloak draped over evil, a monster underneath a flesh-mask? Are they being duped?

X: But what do you think I've done! *(Beat, corrects herself.)* What does the Voice think I've done?

V: Well the facts will be read out in court –

X: What court?

V: The People's Court.

X: I'm being tried? Already? How is this even happening?

V: *(Shocked.)* All proceedings have to take place in a fair and public investigation by The People.

X: But The People aren't telling me what I'm accused of!

V: *(Holds up hands.)* Now. I'm sorry. I can't have shouting. I'm not paid enough for shouting.

X: *(Almost weeping.)* Fuck, I'm sorry, but – this is stressful for me can't you see that? I'm sorry, I'm sorry for shouting, but – I can't understand, I've already been here over three days, I can't call my wife, I can't talk to my children and apparently now I'm on trial for something that nobody can tell me –

V: Oh my dear. You're very scared.

X struggles with tears, breathes rapidly, a panic attack is approaching.

V: Come here.

X sags unwillingly. V moves to put arms around X.

V: That's better. *(Pats X's back.)* Deep breaths. Breathe. And count to eight – and out again. In for eight. Out for eight.

X warily complies.

V: When I had my kids, I had to breathe like this for eighteen hours. Can you imagine! Eighteen fucking hours of squirming and grunting and feeling sick and the midwife

24

wandering around going *Breathe!* Like, just give me the drugs and stop lecturing me, you think you can do better? Come here and do better. That's good. In for eight – out for eight –

X manages to breathe back from panic.

X: Please.

V: What's the matter?

X: What's going on? Why are you –

V: Why am I what?

X: Why do you – keep coming back?

V: Coming back?

X: We – we've met before, I know it, I –

V: Do you have a temperature? *(Checks X's forehead.)* You're a little hot, do you want me to make an application for medical assistance?

X: No – I, okay, why not. Will it help?

V: Help?

X: I mean, will it help my case? If I'm ill shouldn't I be moved somewhere?

V: Well I'm no doctor, but I can do the paperwork. There's a form somewhere. No, wait. Did I bring one? *(Hunts interminably.)*

X: Do you have a phone?

V: A phone?

X: I just want to call my wife. She's going to be so worried, she can't reach me, it's been days now, and –

V: I don't have a phone, I'm afraid.

X: Oh God.

X buries her head in her hands, rocks back and forth. Pause. There is the ping of a notification. X raises head, stares at V.

V: OK *(Spreads hands.) technically* I have a phone, everyone has a phone these days, who doesn't. I think you have to, if you have kids. My oldest, he plays on it all the time.

Pause. X stares appealingly at V.

V: What I meant is, I'm not supposed to –

X: Oh God, please, please, just a quick, a really quick call –

V hesitates.

X: Imagine if you were me, imagine you were in my place –

V: I could get in real trouble for this.

X: I promise, I won't tell a –

V: If the Voice finds out about –

X: Nobody will know. I swear.

V considers, glances over her shoulder, pulls ponderingly at collar. X fidgets anxiously.

V: *(Taking out phone.)* OK, you've got one minute.

X: Oh God, thank you, thank you.

X grapples with phone, nearly drops it in haste, dials number.

V: Careful, it's a new one.

X: Thank you, sorry, fuck *(Gets up and paces.)* Pick up, pick up, pick up.

V stares at her, shaking her head, then gets a paper out of her briefcase and starts to write.

X: *(Pacing.)* Please please FUCK she's not –

V checks her watch, it beeps.

V: Time's up

X: Please, she always answers, just one more –

V: Time's up, you're pushing your luck

X rebelliously re-dials, backs away, it rings again. Finally X exhales in fury, practically throws the phone back to V.

X: Fuck, where is she? Where is she?

X buries head in hands.

X: *(Muttering to herself.)* Where's she gone? Where is she?

V: I said careful, it's new! I haven't had it insured yet.

X: If you break it, say it's lost, with this model you get automatic cover.

V: I do?

X: Yes, with the warranty.

V: Ahhhh.

V fastidiously polishes the screen, breathes on it, polishes.

V: I've got your medical examination form.

X: Okay.

V: It's a recommendation that you be evaluated by a physician and assessed for your illness. You are ill, aren't you?

X: I'm not – *(Catches V's eye.)* yes, yes I am ill.

V: What symptoms do you have?

X: I don't know. I just feel bad.

V: *(Writing.)* Symptoms ... *feel ... bad.* Hmmm. Probably beef that up a bit, but that's probably enough for now. Have you had anything to eat or drink today?

X: I'm not – I don't know.

V: How long have you been detained?

X: Two, three – I can't remember.

V: You need to keep hydrated. Being kept alone like this, it's not good for you. Brings on all sorts of strange thoughts. I've seen it before. You go round and round in your head like a hamster wheel. One boy – nine years old I think he was – chewed his finger off down to the knuckle in his cage. Nasty business. Another lady kept doing her business on the floor. Right over there. Next to the toilet bucket. No reason for it. *(Points.)* There! Right next to the bucket.

X looks, unwillingly.

V: Nasty business. Well, I think I've got everything for now. You'll be told when the date of your hearing has been set, and then we can take it from there. I'll submit your medical form and ask for you to be seen.

X: How long's it going to take?

V: The doctor?

X: The hearing. Everything.

V: Well, the doctor should be fairly quick, but the hearing – well I really wouldn't like to say. There was one guy who – no, I don't think we should talk about him. But, drink water, okay? Lots of water. Keep your mind fresh.

X: You're going?

V: Well our time is up, so –

X: Will you come back again?

V: Again?

X: Will – will *you* come back? You're the first – first person who's – been a bit kind. Thank you.

V: I'm just doing my job. There's thousands like you. Now you stay safe and keep hydrated. *(Leaving.)* And remember to use the bucket.

X: *(Banging on door.)* Wait! Come back! Come back! Please!

SNAP LIGHTS

SCENE 4

An (almost) instant re-entry of V in general's cap; walks X backwards around the room.

V: Just give it up.

X: Give up – what?

V: Drop the act.

X: …

V: You're lying.

X: What – ?

V: We know you're lying.

X: …

V: You're bang to rights on this.

X: Lying about –

V holds up X's phone.

V: Tell us the truth.

X: I did, I –

V: You weren't "solely providing humanitarian assistance" were you?

X: …

V: Just stop the harmless volunteer act for a moment. It's fooling no one.

X: An act?

V: The act.

X: You're one to talk, you –

V: We know who you are

X: Yes, I told you, I'm –

V: You actively engaged in activities and plans which could compromise, destabilise or otherwise threaten –

X: What? I would never –

V: You left water in the wastelands.

X: But – people would have died without –

V: Whole barrels of water on the migrant route.

X: But that's humanitarian –

V: It's only humanitarian in the camps. To registered people. Real people.

X: But – but they're all people.

V: Are they?

X: What?

V: What makes a person?

X: I don't understand.

V: What is a person?

X: Human?

V: To be a person is to be part of The People. And those who are not part of The People – well, you're inciting them to break laws.

X: What?

V: Encouraging them.

X: Nobody – nobody chose to travel because we were leaving water in the mountains. That's just –

V: Incitement. Instigation.

X: What?

V: We have evidence, hard evidence.

X: What evidence?

V: *(Tapping phone.)* In here.

X: My phone?

V: The protests.

X: What about the protests.

V: You videoed them.

X: Hang on, okay, fuck okay, once I filmed a bit – but it wasn't, I didn't know –

V: It was uploaded to external servers that distribute material for the populist uprising in the annexed territories.

X: But – no, that can't be.

V: Why should The People believe anything you say?

X: Because I haven't lied, I haven't –

V: You've never lied to us?

X: I forgot, it was one clip, that's all, and –

V: And uploaded it?

X: I didn't – okay, I sent it to my wife, but –

V: Where were you radicalised? Here, or in the –

X: *(Laughing nervously.)* I'm not a terrorist.

V: Terrorists never call themselves terrorists.

X: I'm not – listen, this is all a huge –

> *X can't stop laughing nervously. V stares at X, X controls self with an effort.*

V: This is a very strange reaction to being called a terrorist.

X: It's just – it's just so absurd, that's –

V: You think terrorists are absurd.

X: I don't – I'm not. *(Struggles with panicked laughter.)*. Look. Whatever you think I am, whatever you're saying I've done, it's not true, that's my story, I'm sticking to it. You know it! Double-flush, casino break, my ace takes your king.

> *Pause. V circles X.*

V: A lot of people come through these doors. A lot. All with the same story. They're innocent. They didn't know. They weren't aware. They never meant any harm.

X: It's true.

V: We've heard it before. Over and over again. The first story. The one you're telling us right now. It sounds reasonable. Appropriate, even. Moderate, and it paints you in a good light. But the interesting thing is, it's never the end story.

X: The end story?

V: The end story is the one they tell when they've nothing else to lose. The one they tell when they really have to.

X: I have no end story –

V: It takes a little while of getting to. It's the story that has to be coaxed out. It's been buried for so long that it's part of you. Perhaps you don't even know it, for so long you've been telling yourself the first story that you've even come to believe it.

X: It's the real –

V steps forward, takes X's hand.

X: What are you doing?

V: It's like a dance. Both partners know where they're going. What steps they're going to take to arrive there. There's the leader and the follower in a game of push-and-pull. *(Assumes dance position, makes X place hands on shoulders and arm. They dance.)* The leader knows all the moves before they're made. They never ask a question to which they don't already know the answer. *(Music.)* The leader knows the footwork, and they always prompt the follower, a second, a millisecond before they need to turn, or change direction. Like this. *(Pushes on X's hand for a turn, performs a creditable chaine pass.)*

The follower knows what the leader is about. Their job is to follow, to respond to the change in tempo, the altered hand clasp that tells them, it's time to turn now. They can't anticipate. They mustn't, otherwise the dance doesn't work.

You don't want a mess that trips everyone up, do you? There's people watching, after all.

They dance for a while.

X: Why – why do you think I've got a real story?

V: Everybody always has. Getting to the real story is a bit like giving birth. There's a lot of fear at first. Maybe a lot of confusion. And then – a lot of pain. A pain that you don't think you can ever get out of.

Beat.

V: But then – then the pain reaches a peak. The crowning. The real story starts to emerge. Tentatively, because it wants to stay inside, inside where it's safer. It's not used to coming out. Being seen.

But once it emerges – it all starts to become easier. Much easier. A few pushes, and – And very soon – the real story comes out. Finally. And all that fear and pain was for nothing. You see?

V steps back, breaking the dance.

X: You're threatening me?

V: I'm just the voice of experience here.

X: I want to see a lawyer.

V: You've seen a lawyer.

X: I saw you! You came in here, pretending to be a lawyer, I know, I know, I know what you're doing, you're trying to play with my mind, this is some kind of weird psycho strategy, but I'm not stupid. I want to see another lawyer, a proper one.

V: In cases of terrorism, the usual rights are –

X: I'm not a terrorist!

V: There's people – many people like you – who disappear.

X: Threats, threats, it's all threats. I'm not a terrorist, your say-so doesn't make it the –

V: Okay, you want to play hard ball now?

X: I'm not hardball, I'm telling you, I'm telling you –

V steps forward, holding out hands.

V: Let's dance.

X is terrified, but stands upright, takes V's arm. They dance, music fails, scratches to dissonance.

X stands in stress position.

SNAP LIGHTS

SCENE 5

X is sitting, stiff and obviously in pain.

V is dressed as a doctor in white coat, kneeling next to X, checking blood pressure, etc, calm and methodical.

V: I don't think it's broken. There's no swelling or contusions that I can see.

X: I can't move – around my shoulder.

V: It's not broken.

X: But I can't use it.

V: If it's not broken, I shall certify that no international laws have been contravened.

X: It won't work.

V: How about the other one?

X tries to move other arm.

X: It kind of works, but there's a lump.

V: A lump?

X: Just under here.

V: *(Measuring.)* It's under three inches, which is the authorised limit to EIT[1] affects under the current administration, so I can still certify this as legal.

X: This is legal?

V: Use of EITs are authorised in cases of national emergency.

X: But – how do you think this happened?

V: Well let's look at the statement itself, shall we. You attempted to self-injure yourself but were prevented –

X: You believe that?

V: *(Repeating.)* Well let's look at the statement itself, shall we –

X: You think I did this myself?

V: I've seen worse in here. A lot worse.

X: I didn't –

V: You think this is bad? I saw one guy with all his blood pooled in one place. His heart was hardly beating. All his muscles had ceased to function. That's what you need to worry about. When you cease to function. Are you still functioning?

X: Well, yes, but –

---

1   Enhanced Interrogation Techniques (i.e. not classed as torture officially.)

Y: You look like you're functioning.

X: Listen –

V: Let me check your pulse. *(Holds wrist, counts.)*

X: So you're a doctor now, are you?

V: I'm sorry?

X: You're playing a doctor now?

V: *(Adjusts stethoscope.)* Can you breathe out please, I need to check your lungs.

V moves the stethoscope over X's chest. X stares at the ceiling.

X: I get how this goes. This is the good-cop bit. Then in a while you'll come back and play the bad cop role again.

V: How long have you been feeling this way?

X: Feeling what way?

V: Do you often feel that you've seen someone before?

X: I know – when I've seen someone before, and they're telling me I haven't. I know when I'm being tricked.

V: Do you often feel that people are out to get you? Trip you up, trap you?

X laughs mirthlessly.

X: I *know* I've seen you before.

V: I had an old man that thought I was his mother, once. He'd walked all the way from the war zone and he'd lost all his medication on the way. Thought he was eight years old again. Used to hang on to my arm and cry when I gave him an injection. *(Beat.)* How long have you been incarcerated?

X: A few weeks? Twenty days? I don't know, I don't see sunlight, I don't have a clock, it's just a guess.

V: Are you receiving regular food?

X: Well it's food, but –

V: You're in Category X cell. The food and privileges in Category V cells are better.

X: Are you going to move me there?

V: I don't think that's possible right now.

X: Why not? I'm sick, you said it yourself, I'm ill.

V: You haven't changed your story for days.

X: Why should I change it?

V puts away stethoscope, considers.

V: If you give them something – even a little thing – it can make all the difference.

X: What?

V: You're then classed as a "co-operating prisoner." You get cells with windows. Hot food. Exercise for an hour a day.

X: Grass myself up, you mean.

V measures X's wrists, ankles etc.

V: You're quite underweight, are you eating and drinking properly?

X: You should know, you're behind it, you're behind this whole thing.

Pause. V marks up a chart.

V: I've seen a lot of people in your position.

X: What position?

V: Good people getting co-opted into a bad cause. It's a really, really common story.

X: I'm not a terrorist

V: Girl in my year went off to help on the front lines when we graduated. Next I knew she was up in court for trafficking people. Claimed she did it for nothing so it wasn't illegal. They didn't believe her, though. Why would you do all that for free?

X: …

V: You thought you were working for a good cause.

X: I was just – helping people.

V: It's understandable. You see injustice – or how you perceive it. You go out there – you want to help. You absorb ideas. You take on the perspective that people are telling you.

X: It is injust! Un – unjust. What they're doing out there. There's none of it on the TV. Nothing on the radio.

V: Have you heard of basic assumptions –the filter through which we view the world. If we feel people are essentially untrustworthy, then we find betrayal in every action, no matter how innocent.

X: This isn't a basic assumption.

V: And of course then there's confirmatory bias – if we're expecting to see something, we see it. You know?

X: I saw things with my own eyes out there. Terrible things.

V: The world is full of terrible things, but –

X: I didn't make them up. I saw them. They're true, they're real. And I wanted to help.

V: You keep coming back to that.

X: To what?

V: Help. You wanted to help.

X: Yes. What's wrong with that.

V: It's all very, very common. Most volunteers are actually running from something, they say. They're unhappy within themselves, so they seek out a challenging environment to give them a sense of purpose. A sense of being needed.

X: So helping people is selfish now?

V: Helping releases endorphins, the things that make us feel good. It's a natural chemical bonding for a group that keeps it together, makes it cohesive.

X: Okay, so what, so what if I was unhappy at home? So what if I went out and helped people worse off than me? Does it make it a bad thing? Does it make it not true?

V: I'm just trying to unpick what made you go out there in the first place. You said you were unhappy at home.

X: I wasn't unhappy at home, I said, *so what if* –

V: Were you unhappy at home?

X: OK, I wasn't unhappy, but I was – not happy enough. Like, I felt that everything back home was an illusion, what we were being told – wasn't – *it*. Wasn't – true. That there was a whole world underneath us where – bad things are happening, while we were sitting on the top one per cent, and it's like an iceberg where you can't see below, can't see below the surface, but you know it's there, but everyone at the top pretends it's not happening, that everything's fine, and – I had to go out, I had to see for myself.

V: The things you saw out there, they affected you?

X: Affected – well of course, yes

V: Made you feel angry?

X: Angry, yes, because out there I saw people – people living with nothing, in mud, on our borders, because of the occupation, while in here we were all agonising about which of the twenty types of latte we were going to drink that morning.

V: You were angry

X: I don't know how any sane person isn't angry.

V: You feel yourself to be a sane person.

X: I am sane.

V: Right.

X: I am sane.

V: So despite recognising people that you've never seen before, you feel yourself to be sane.

X: I – trust my own eyes. Yes.

V: This anger you're feeling was against –

X: Well, the way things were. Are. I was angry about – how it's all set up.

V: You see, it's natural. This confusion. It helps to see both sides, to get your head round it.

X: Both sides.

V: There's another way that this anger could be directed. Anger towards those who hate our freedoms and wish us harm. Anger towards those who send others to protest by stirring up trouble while they sit at home. Anger towards people who ask others to wear their suicide belts.

X: So all this is someone else's fault?

V: We can't save everyone. But the people we can save, they're right here, with us. The People give ourselves the freedom. Twenty types of Latte if we want. That's freedom.

X: Freedom to starve babies in cages?

V: Not our babies.

X sighs.

V: Listen. You were of The People. You were part of us. Out there – they are not. And neither are you. *(Pause.)* I'm trying to give you – give you this chance – to be part of us again.

X: I'm not changing my story.

V: Why not?

X: Because it's – I don't have anything else.

V: You'd be surprised.

Exit V.

X picks up the toilet bucket, flings it around.

X is restrained and tied to a chair.

SNAP LIGHTS

SCENE 6

V enters in black overalls carrying a tool bag. X is tied to a chair.

V: You staged a dirty protest.

X: I – I lost my temper

V: A dirty protest

   This means your existing privileges are revoked.

X: What privileges? I don't have any –

V: The privilege of movement has been revoked until further
   notice.

X: I'm not going to do it again, I just –

V: Until further notice, unless you cooperate.

X: I'm cooperating.

V: When were you recruited?

X: I wasn't – I'm not recruited.

V: Doing all this out of the goodness of your heart?

X: I've said, I've told you guys – I wanted to help.

V: You wanted to be a superhero?

X: Not – just try, really, helping.

V: Why did you want to help?

X: I saw, I saw what was going on, and –

V: How did you see "what was going on"?

X: Well –

V: Who showed you?

X: I – I just

V: Who showed you?

X: Nobody showed me, it was just my wife came across it, and
she said, look at this, what a shame, those poor people,
and – after that, I couldn't stop thinking about it.

V: So your wife showed you.

X: No, leave her out of it, it was just looking, just looking
really –

V: Did you argue with your wife?

X: Argue? Who doesn't?

V: What did you argue about?

X: Stuff. I can't remember. The way she used to chew her
food? Stupid things. Couple things.

V: Did you argue about the children? Her children?

X: No?

V: Get on well with the children? Even though they weren't
yours?

X: What does that have to do with –

V: Did you love your wife?

X: Yes, but, you can hate and love at the same time, can't
you? Like you can't bear to look at someone for one single
second and yet you'd still jump in front of a train to save
them?

V: And yet you still filed for divorce.

Beat.

X: How do you know that?

V: Did you or did you not file for divorce.

X: Well – okay, things had got bad, so we – we went for mediation and counselling and then we decided to stay together, and we realised that we could be better –

V: Why should we believe anything you say?

X: I don't know.

V: You bribed your lawyer

X: I didn't, I only –

V: You asked to use her phone.

X: It was – no, it was your phone, you came here, you said you were a lawyer, you –

V: You used her phone.

X: So this was a trap, it's all entrapment? You come in here, time after time, pretending to be different people, and –

V: You used her phone to call an active agent.

X: What? I just tried to call my –

V: She isn't your wife.

   Beat.

X: *(Stunned.)* An active –

V: An active agent operating to overthrow The People from within.

X: …

V: An active agent who you falsely said to your legal representative was your wife.

X: Oh God. This –

V: Why are you laughing?

X: I'm not laughing – yes I am, because it's all gone mad, you're lying, it's you, you're the ones lying.

V: She's an identified active agent that has been working you for years.

X: No. No, this is ridiculous.

V: You've been groomed. Used. Emotionally manipulated.

X: You – no, you don't understand, my wife has never left The People, she was here all the time, if you think she's an enemy agent you've got her confused with someone else.

V: What did you actually do during your time in the annexe?

X: I told you! I'm –

V: A volunteer, yes you keep saying, but *(Taps phone.)* we've discredited that so –

X: It's true, it's true, I –

V: You were recruited, groomed, and indoctrinated by the underground terrorist network seeking to disrupt the safety and security of The People.

X: This is laughable, it's a farce –

V: You filmed a lot of classified material.

X: No, it was just one protest –

V: There's thousands of gig of film on your phone.

X: There's what?

V: Thousands of images contrary to your statement at the beginning of your investigation which could compromise, destabilise or otherwise threaten the security of The

People, their citizens, institutions or democracy, now or in the future.

X: Wait, no, I'll show you, there's only one, and I didn't *(Grabs for phone, tries to flick through it.)* What – what is this?

V: You should know

X: I don't – this isn't, this isn't mine, I never took these.

V: It's the phone we took from you to analyse.

X: No, no it can't be.

V: Let's drop the act, shall we?

X: I don't understand. This must have been put on here, afterwards –

V: You're accusing The People of planting evidence?

X: Someone must have! I never had any –

V: Thank you.

From V's bag she lays out a line of instruments on the desk, pliers, a small hand-held drill, a screwdriver, etc.

X: What – what are you doing?

V: Remember what I told you about the hidden story?

X: What?

V: The end story? The story that's buried somewhere, and like diviners, we have to follow the course of the water to where it is.

X: You're going to –

V: I'm showing you that it's not worth it.

X wriggles but cannot move. V clicks the hand held drill, holds it aloft, gives it a few experimental spins.

X: What. Oh God. No.

V: Right now, we're stuck on the first story. We can't move, we're in checkmate. But the thing about the first story is that it's an illusion. It might look real, but it can be taken apart. It seems solid, but after a little experiment – a little enquiry – we start to see that it's not.

X: What you're suggesting – it's not true, it's not, it's lies –

V: Everything gets reduced to its component parts. What seemed so strong and solid now lies in pieces. We see it as the fiction that it is.

X: Don't – don't you touch me –

V kneels down, applies the drill to the table, withdraws a screw, pockets it.

V: The first lie comes out. *(Shakes table.)* Already the story is unbalanced. *(Drills out another screw.)* Look. One of the legs comes off really easily, but the other one sticks. *(Uses pliers to take out the second screw.)* This lie is stubborn. It needs pulling out. *(Removes screw.)* Now look. Two pillars of the story are gone, and it's useless.

X: You're not going to –

V: You see how easily something can be deconstructed. To get at the truth. That an elaborate fantasy can be taken down so, so easily.

X: Don't you touch me.

V stands up, looks at X, spins the drill.

X: Don't you touch me!

V spins the drill. X screams.

THE STORYTELLER: *You're doing very well.*

Now tell us what happened next.

There's always a next. We're connected.

There's things within us that we don't even know,

Things we never thought of, things that haven't even taken shape,

The formless things that mouths never uttered,

The truths we never thought of, history that was never spoken,

It's up to you to birth it.

Breathe, breathe,

Count 1 to 8,

You'll find it if you're searching,

There's always something to search for. A journey

Of light in the darkness, the first spark

That leads you towards understanding,

The memory that makes you sit up, like a child on a summer morning

And say – oh, yes, *now I remember* –

SNAP LIGHTS

SCENE 7

X has a bag on her head, still tied to the chair.

V enters in NGO lanyard and civvies and carrying a clipboard. She is nervous, shy, the aspect of an eager worker on her first job.

V: Good morning! I hope I'm not too late. *(Stands, uncertainly.)* Did they let you know I was coming?

Pause. X moves to signify consciousness very slightly.

V: I've been assigned yourself as an individual worthy of observation. *(Checks notes, reads from script in sing-song phone-interview manner.)* I'm a legal observer working on the border here, and we're in charge of making sure that all prisoners, no matter which category they are, are kept in accordance with the conventions governing international incarceration.

Pause. X turns towards her.

V: You are … Prisoner X, right?

X nods.

V: It does feel odd not being on first-name terms. I don't think I'll ever get used to it. *(Looks around for somewhere to sit.)* I'll tell you a bit about myself to break the ice shall I? *(Pause.)* I've been employed for a month now overseeing incarceration facilities at the border to make sure they're in line with international law. We're all assigned detainees to interview, one of which is yourself. I also like modern dance, fishing, and the novels of Virginia Woolf.

Pause.

V: I have to say, it's a little exciting. You're the highest-ranked prisoner that I've ever interviewed. I don't think I've ever had a Category X before. I'm kind of in awe.

Pause.

V: I'm afraid I'm not able to ask about your personal circumstances because we have to stick to the script, but I can confirm, now, that I've seen yourself, okay, and now I'm putting a tick in the box *(Ticks.)* that says you're here, you exist, and that you are available for interview today.

Pause.

V: So I have a few questions here, would you like to start?

Pause.

V: Are you happy to be interviewed by myself today? These kind of questions are on a script and they're a yes/no or a 1 – 10 format.

Pause.

X: 10.

V: Aha, my bad sorry, these kind of questions are on a script and they're a yes/no or a 1 – 10 format, so I'll repeat, are you happy to be interviewed by myself today, yes or no?

X: Yes.

V: On a scale of 1 – 10, how would you class the food and facilities here, with 10 being the most satisfactory, and 1 being the least satisfactory.

Pause.

V: On a scale of 1 – 10 –

X: I know your voice.

Pause.

V: You know my –

X: I know your voice.

V: Right. I'm afraid, that under the conventions governing international and humane incarceration, we have to stick to the script, so it's either yes/no or a 1 – 10 format, so I'll just repeat, *(Reads.)* "how would you class the food and facilities here, with 10 being the most satisfactory, and 1 being the least satisfactory."

Pause.

X: 1.

V: That's a 1?

X: Yes.

V: So, very, very bad.

X: 1.

V: That's a yes.

X: ... Yes.

V: On the same scale of 1 – 10, how would you class your emotional health and wellbeing today.

X: 1.

V: That's a 1?

X: Yes.

V: Could you now rank the following statements from 1 – 10, with 10 being "most true" and 1 being "not at all or barely true."

I have access to daylight.

I have access to medical support, human company and one hour a day exercise –

X: Why are you doing this?

V: I'm sorry?

X: I know it's always you.

V: I'm afraid we have to stick to the –

X: Fuck you and fuck your script. Fuck your one to tens. Fuck your yeses. Fuck your *yourselves.* *(Tries to shunt chair closer to V.)* Coming round here trying to pretend everything is fine with your little clipboard so everyone can feel better –

V: I'm afraid that if we continue like this that I'm going to have to terminate the interview.

X: Shut up you useless little piece of shit!

V: That's so insulting. You can't speak to me like that! I'm a person! I have feelings!

X: *(Laughing hysterically.)* Just fuck off. Fuck off!

V: Interview terminated 11.15.

V runs out of the room in tears. X falls to the ground laughing and convulsing.

The weeping continues.

SNAP LIGHTS

SCENE 8

X sits on the floor, tied up, hooded.

V sits beside her, a hood also over her head, weeping.

V: Why? Why are you doing this?

X: What?

V: Oh God. Stop it, stop it, stop it.

X sits up, wriggles away.

X: What? What's happening?

V: It's me.

X: Who?

V: Your cellmate.

X: What cellmate?

V: You know.

X recoils.

V: Why are you doing this? Why are you doing this to all of us?

X: What? Who are you?

V: Are you really going to play this with me now?

X: Play? What the fuck!

V: You're pretending you don't know me.

X: I don't know you, listen –

V: You abandoned me.

X: I'm not, I'm not doing this.

V: You have to speak, you have to.

X: Who are – this is a joke, right, a –

V: You need to tell them.

X: This is a set-up.

V: You know me.

X: I don't know you.

V: You know my voice.

Pause. Change of attitude from V.

V: It's nicer in here. You've got your own space. The other cells, they're overcrowded. You lie with your head between someone's knees, they have their head in someone else's. You breathe in their stink. The food – well, I can't even begin to describe it. Rotten and germinated, like some kind of worm-barrel.

Pause.

V: I've been here for a long time. Maybe longer than you. I don't know when you were taken. A month? Two months?

X: I don't know.

V: I've missed you.

X: I don't miss you because I don't know you.

V: You do know me.

X: Shut up!

V: I'm just trying to help you.

X: No!

V: I'm trying to help you out of here.

X: Stop. Stop.

V: I've been in the dark cell. I've seen it. You don't want to go in there, believe me. Scratching a line on the wall every day is an achievement. At least you think it's every day. You're not sure, really. It might be every ten hours, if you don't see sunlight. Or less. So you gain days. Whole weeks and months if you're lucky. You're a time traveller. You're of the future. Superhuman.

X: I'm not listening.

V: But there's some things even superhumans can't manage. There's other things in the darkness. The itching that turns into a pricking that turns into white-hot heat. The heat that won't go away. The frayed nerve-endings. The synaptic shocks. The feedback loop of pain and waking that goes around, over and over and over. Normally you'd pass out – the body would go into shock and relieve you, however temporary, of the nightmare. But here, there's drugs, there's medicines, that make you live again, make you feel everything, all over again, more intensely, more excruciatingly –

X: There's nothing to tell. Nothing.

V: There's plenty to tell. About the wheel and the flying carpet, the electric stun-shocks and the metal chairs. The glass flasks and the biters and being hung up like a ghost. Piece by piece of you being dismantled, death by a thousand cuts, while you watch it happen, on a thousand screens, from every angle.

Pause.

X: Who are you?

V: Have you ever been to the camp at Llanrhaedr?

X: You know I have.

V: You'll have seen me then.

X: I don't know you. I don't.

V: I've been buried.

X: What?

V: You dug a hole and threw me in. Covered me with earth. Buried deep.

X: I don't know what you're talking about, I don't –

V: I've been here. All the time. Waiting for you. Waiting to be discovered.

Beat.

V: Why did you leave?

X: I – I had to go home.

V: You left us?

X: I couldn't – I couldn't do it anymore.

V: We were doing something good. Something worthwhile. But you left. You ran away.

X: I didn't run away. I had enough.

Y: I can't believe it.

X: Everybody has enough at some point.

V: We could have changed things. We could have changed everything.

X: I don't know what you're talking about.

V: We were so close, we had it within our grasp.

X: You're, this is a trick, trying to trap me again, you're saying I was part of – I'm not –

V: You left us, you left our friends. You were part of us. You believed in something. Why don't you believe it now?

X: I don't know what you're saying.

V: You do, you do. You have to say it. Just – say it.

X: I can't say it.

V: You can. Just give them something. About the parcels – you remember them? The things you collected? Dropped off? The people in the back of your van? Something little. Just – something.

X: I never did that.

V: We all did that.

X: This isn't – you're not, you're not real, you can't be.

V: I am real. I always have been.

X: You're not real!

V: Tell me what you remember

X: I don't remember anything!

V: Just tell them the truth.

X: You're not the truth!

V: I'm here, aren't I?

X: Shut up.

V: You have to tell them about me! You have to say what we did!

X: I – we didn't, we – nothing happened!

V: Tell them about the bag! Tell them where you left it! Tell them about the smells of carbon and plastic and how many people disappeared in that crater!

X: This is insane –

V: The stench of a battlefield? Unburnt petroleum, charred plastic, rotten meat, and the sweet candy-floss smell of phosphorous?

X: I don't know, I can't –

V: You can't keep me silent.

X: Tell them what!

V: Tell them what you did!

X: I did nothing, I –

V: That's a lie! If you won't tell them, I will.

X: You're blackmailing me?

V: It's the only way.

X: The only way to lie?

V: The only way to live.

THE STORYTELLER: The story is a work of art.

A beautiful creation,

A weaving, a painting,

Threaded between itself, formed of skeins of memory,

Moulded and shaped by unseen hands,

A museum piece for an unseen audience,

In a darkened gallery.

A word, a glance, a forgotten prompt

Daubed and gilded for the viewer

Into a thing of beauty.

From something that never was,

Never could be,

Born into existence,

The only thing that matters,

The story is inviolable.

SNAP LIGHTS

SCENE 9

X is sleeping. Enter V in civvies, watches her.

V: *(In THE STORYTELLER's voice.)* Good, good.

> You're doing very well.

> Now tell us what happened next.

> *V kneels down, strokes X's hair. X wakes.*

X: What?

V: It's me.

X: *(Beat.)* Oh my god.

> *They embrace.*

V: They wouldn't let me see you.

X: How did you get in?

V: I waited for so long. I kept going back day after day. I called everyone I knew. They said they couldn't help. I paid money. I paid bribes. I offered sex. They passed me around. I mortgaged the house. The kids have to stay at my mother's. I tried three bribes, each one bigger than the last. I don't have enough money for another one.

X: I'm sorry.

V: It doesn't matter.

X: I don't know what to do.

V: You're going to have to give me up.

X: I'm not going to give you up.

V: You will.

X: I don't want to.

V: It doesn't matter.

X: You're the only thing that matters.

Pause.

X: I always knew it was you. Always.

V: What?

X: No matter who comes, who speaks to me, I always see the same face. Do you understand? It's the same face. They might be high-up, low down, general or pen-pusher, but they've always got the same face. The same voice.

V: I know.

X: I can only ever see your face.

V: It's OK.

X: I don't know what it means, I don't understand.

V: You don't have to understand.

X: They want me to –

V: I know.

X: I can't say it. I can't.

V: You can use my voice. Use my face.

X: I can't.

V: Of course you can.

X: It's not true.

V: Of course it is.

X: None of this is true. Only you are.

V: Just tell the truth.

X: I don't know the truth anymore.

V: Just tell them.

Pause.

X: I'm going to tell them the real story.

V: You're going to change your statement?

X: I'm going to change my statement.

V: To indict me?

X: Yes.

V: Why now? Why should they believe you?

X: Because it's the – listen, I couldn't say it at first, but, it's the –

V: So you're going to play ball?

X: I'm going to play ball.

V: Or are you going to tell them another lie?

X: I promise, I promise promise promise that I'm telling the truth.

V: Why now, after all this time?

X: I was scared, don't you get it?

V: Scared of –

X: You.

V: Me.

X: I was just a pawn. Like in chess, I didn't know, I swear, I didn't know until it was all just too much.

V takes a step forward, spins X into position.

V: And then?

X: Well, it didn't start with much, just people asking me –

V: Pawns take two steps on their first move.

X takes two steps. With each line, each of them make a chess move, circling each other.

V: What happened next?

X: Bringing parcels here and there.

V: Explosives?

X: Yes.

V: With intent to maim, kill or cause serious injury?

X: Yes.

V: You were aware of this?

X: Yes.

V: How were you aware of this?

X: I was a pawn.

V: You keep saying, but a pawn of whom?

X: Of you.

V: You'll need more details. Evidence.

X: I can get evidence.

V: You're doing very well.

Pause.

X: You're not my wife.

V: Who am I?

X: My recruiter.

V: For how long?

X: Years.

V: Was that how we started?

X: Yes.

V: What did I make you do?

X: You fed me propaganda. You showed me fake news. You
filled my head with your story. You made me do things I
never wanted to.

V: Like?

X: You know – you know – you gave me packages. Smelling
of marzipan and candy-floss.

V: What do you want?

X: I want to be of The People again.

V: You want to come back to us?

X: Yes.

V: Then give us something. What will you give us?

X: You.

X steps forward, takes V by the hand. Dance. Darkness, music.

SNAP LIGHTS

SCENE 10

V is in the chair wearing the prison shift. X stands.

V: Listen, it's not you saying these things, it can't be –

X: You seem stressed. Why are you stressed if there's nothing
to hide?

V: There's nothing – nothing! I would never – I would never do that.

X: You did. You knew it.

V: I loved you. I tried everything to get you back –

X: It's not enough. Love is never enough.

V: I rang and rang and rang, I waited in queues, I hocked favours, I asked everyone, I went to the press, I –

X: You recruited me.

V: I never, never did.

X: Where were you radicalised? Where did you build your network?

V: I'm not a terrorist

X: That's a very strange way of reacting to being called a terrorist.

V: It's me – it's me! You know this! Why are you saying these things!

X: It's the truth.

V: They've got to you, haven't they!

X: You recruited me, groomed me, and made me one of your messengers.

V: I can't – what are you saying?

X: And the children.

V: What – what about the children?

X: They ran packages and left them where they were told. I mean, who would ever think to search a child?

V: No, stop, stop saying this – they're eight, just eight years old –

X: There's no age limit for terrorism.

V: My children – our children – they'd never, why, why are you doing this to them, it's all lies, all lies.

X: You tried to make me forget, but I remember.

V: You would give up your children – your own children, to save yourself?

X: They're not children. They're not people.

V: Fuck, you've gone crazy, you're not in your right mind, really, really –

X: I remember everything.

V: It's a story, you made up a story, you –

X: I'm speaking to save us. All of us.

V: Save us –

X: I'm of The People. I'm speaking for The People.
(Kneels down.) If you confess it, if you just let yourself acknowledge – for one minute –

V: It's not true, though.

X: Everything is true.

V: Even the things that can't possibly be true? Two opposites?

X: It's all true.

V: Stories that cancel each other out?

X: Especially those! There are the moments they are true, and in other moments there are others that are truer. You can only say one story at a time, though. And that's the one that occupies the space. The story that occupies the voice, the mouth that speaks it, the words it uses, it's all true.

V: But you can't – you can't say that we were terrorists, you can't say that the children were terrorists –

X: Once it's said, it's real.

V: Nothing about this is real!

X: You've got one minute to think it over.

V: There isn't *(Laughing nervously.)* this isn't –

X: Why are you laughing?

V: Because, because – because –

V laughs hysterically, fades.

THE STORYTELLER: It's the same voice

Coming from the next room

Thickened through walls, distorted by corners,

A conversation by grown-ups

When you're only eight and you're frightened,

The words say one thing, but the tone says another.

There's something else going on but you're not sure,

Like the subtext when someone says *I'm fine* and

Their voice says but *my husband killed himself on Wednesday,*

And *that's life though*, and *got to keep on keeping on,*

The words make no sense but you know who's saying them,

You hear the tone behind them that says, *no, no, no,*

The sound that lends the lie to everything.

But once the story is birthed, it's true.

Like the history of empires

Written by conquerors

It occupies the space that was vacant,

Its seeds start to germinate,

And even if the branches are cut down later

The roots are spreading.

SNAP LIGHTS

SCENE 11

V is fidgeting nervously on the chair in civvies. Glances nervously at clock. Echoes of the first scene.

X enters in lanyard/ border force cap, harassed.

X: Sorry to keep you waiting, we've been –

V: It's fine, really.

X: Nightmare workload today, nightmare.

V: Yes, it's fine.

X: Drink?

V: Well –

X: Great, let's plunge right in, this is the awkward bit, I have to read this in full we can do some box-ticking; it's a bit of a mouthful, but anyway *(Reads.)* "Are you now, or have you ever been, engaged in any activity or plans which could compromise, destabilise or otherwise threaten the security of The People, their citizens, institutions or democracy, now or in the future?"

V: No.

X: Why are you staring?

V: It's weird but – you really reminded me of someone for a moment there. I can't think who, though.

X: Really?

V: Yes, just – it's so strange.

X: Probably the uniform. We all look the same to you guys, huh.

V: No, it's not that – it's – it feels like I should recognise you but I don't. Like seeing someone who's moved away, or changed their hair or something. You get the flash of a face, or the way someone moves, or the way they smell, and it's familiar, but also strange, kind of bewildering –

X: Really?

V: Yes.

X: I only started this job last week, so I don't see –

V: It's – it's uncanny. Like I should know you, but I don't. Like a long-lost sister or a brother. Or someone's child, when you see the features of their parents in their face but they're different somehow, they're mixed round, like the eyes should be one colour but they're another, but for all that, they've got exactly the same expression –

X: You sound a bit stressed.

V: Well okay, I'm very stressed, I've been here for –

X: Do you want to take my advice?

V: Um, okay.

X: Stress doesn't look good.

V: It's just, you keep asking me lots of questions, and –

X: But we've only just started.

V: No, you've talked to me before. A few days ago, I can't remember.

X: *(Startled.)* Me?

V: Yes. And a few days before that.

X: Honestly, I think you're a little confused.

V: I'm not confused. I see you. I know – I know who you are.

X: You do?

V: Yes

X: Who am I then?

V: You're – you've got the same face. The same voice. You keep coming back. And I keep talking to you, but you – you forget. You forget what you've heard. What you've done. Like you've forgotten yourself.

X: Well, I don't think I –

V: I see the same face.

The face that's underneath every cap, above every type of uniform. I hear the same voice that keeps asking different things. The same face I see playing on the cricket pitch, the same face that hands out supplies in camps, the same face that stands on the border squinting down a rifle to shoot the kids with the same faces when they play too close. The voice on TV that tells us that people with faces just like yours are coming to kill us, that they hate our freedoms, that people with the same face are the reason that people with faces like you are suffering, because people with the same face have taken it all away.

Beat.

X: Look. I like you. I believe you're a good person –

V: I am a good person!

X: – but I'm going to have to terminate this interview now –

V: Don't you understand?

X: I'll have my superior come to interview you, because –

V: It'll be you. You'll go out of that door, and come back, and it'll be you, but it won't be you, because you'll have forgotten everything, but I'll know it's you, because –

X: Listen –

V: You'll have the same face, the same voice. Saying different words because you don't know what you've done, you don't remember what you've learned, you just repeat everything, over and over again.

X: I'm going to have to –

V: Until now.

I know you.

V reaches out, touches X's face.

V: Will you listen to me now?

Will you hear me now?

Will you remember who you are?

END OF PLAY

www.ingramcontent.com/pod-product-compliance
Ingram Content Group UK Ltd.
Pitfield, Milton Keynes, MK11 3LW, UK
UKHW020739280225
455688UK00013B/744

9 781786 829344